Crayola World of ORANGE

Mari Schuh

Lerner Publications ◆ Minneapolis

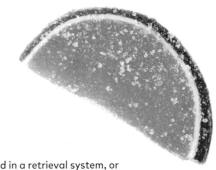

For the amazing second-grade students
at St. John Vianney School

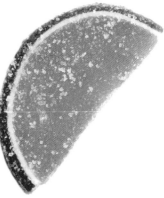

Official Licensed Product
Lerner Publications Company
A division of Lerner Publishing Group, Inc.
241 First Avenue North
Minneapolis, MN 55401 USA

For reading levels and more information, look up this title at www.lernerbooks.com.

Main body text set in Mikado a Medium 20/28.
Typeface provided by HVD Fonts.

Library of Congress Cataloging-in-Publication Data

Names: Schuh, Mari C., 1975- author. | Crayola (Firm)
Title: Crayola world of orange / by Mari Schuh.
Other titles: World of orange
Description: Minneapolis : Lerner Publications, [2020]. | Series: Crayola world of color | Audience: Ages 5-9. | Audience: K to grade 3. | Includes bibliographical references and index.
Identifiers: LCCN 2018038327 (print) | LCCN 2018039297 (ebook) | ISBN 9781541561380 (eb pdf) | ISBN 9781541554702 (lb : alk. paper)
Subjects: LCSH: Orange (Color)—Juvenile literature. | Color in nature—Juvenile literature. | Colors—Juvenile literature. | Crayons—Juvenile literature.
Classification: LCC QC495.5 (ebook) | LCC QC495.5 .S3687225 2020 (print) | DDC 535.6—dc23

LC record available at https://lccn.loc.gov/2018038327

Manufactured in the United States of America
1-45788-42670-12/7/2018

CONTENTS

Hello, Orange!

Orange fills our world.

Peach, burnt orange, and tangerine are shades of orange.
When you look around, where do you see orange?

Orange in Nature

Goodbye, sun!

Orange fills the big, wide sky. Beautiful sunsets mark the end of the day.

Orange glides from the trees.
Leaves change color in fall.
Winter will be here soon!

Orange Animals

See **orange** flutter through the garden. Monarch butterflies sip nectar from flowers. Then they fly away!

Orange cats are fluffy and soft. Thick fur keeps them warm.

Meow!

Orange explores the rain forest. Orangutans hang out in the trees. What will they see?

Orange Foods

Look up!

Oranges grow on fruit trees. They are sweet and juicy!

17

Look down!

Carrots grow under the ground.
These crunchy vegetables are
tasty and good for you.

Orange Where You Live

You can see **orange** in many sports. Go out and have some fun!

People wear **orange** life
jackets near water.
Be safe and enjoy the lake!

Orange is bright.
Workers wear safety
vests and hats.
Bright colors make them
easy to see.

Orange is hard at work! Strong machines scoop, lift, and haul. Race cars speed around the track.

What other places can you find *orange*?

Color with Orange!

Draw a fun picture using only orange crayons. What will you draw? How many shades of orange will you use?

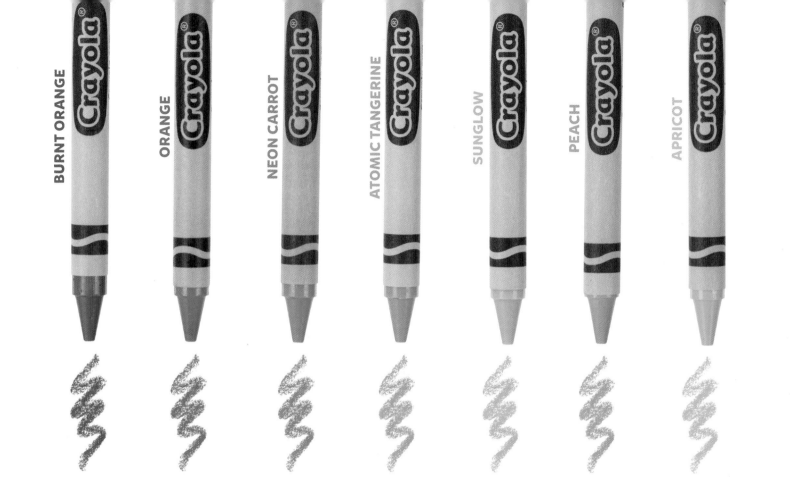

BURNT ORANGE

ORANGE

NEON CARROT

ATOMIC TANGERINE

SUNGLOW

PEACH

APRICOT

Orange All around You

Orange is found around the world. Here are some Crayola® crayon shades of **orange** used in this book. Can you find them in the photos? Which **orange** is your favorite?

Glossary

explore: to look around an area

flutter: quickly flapping wings to fly

haul: to move something heavy

nectar: a sweet liquid made by many plants

orangutan: a large ape

shade: the lightness or darkness of a color

vegetable: a plant that is eaten for food

To Learn More

Books

Leaf, Christina. *Orange Animals*. Minneapolis: Bellwether Media, 2019.
Explore the color orange by reading about orange animals.

Schuh, Mari. *Crayola Fall Colors*. Minneapolis: Lerner Publications, 2018.
Enjoy all the colors you can find during fall, including the color orange!

Websites

Crayola Coloring Page: Jack-o'-Lanterns
https://www.crayola.com/free-coloring-pages/print/jack-o-lanterns-coloring
-page/
Visit this website to color several fun jack-o'-lanterns.

Kid Zone: Orange Coloring Page
http://www.kidzone.ws/prek_wrksht/colors/ib-book-orange.htm
Use your orange crayons to color orange objects.

Index

Photo Acknowledgments

Image credits: olgaman/Shutterstock.com, p. 2; TFoxFoto/Shutterstock.com, p. 4 (pumpkins); kariphoto/Shutterstock.com, p. 4 (cut squash); Amawasri Pakdara/Shutterstock.com, p. 4 (popsicle); Dave King/Dorling Kindersley/Getty Images, p. 5 (tiger); Mark Herreid/Shutterstock.com, p. 5 (sunset); DCornelius/Shutterstock.com, p. 6; Evgeny Dubinchuk/Shutterstock.com, pp. 6–7; A Periam Photography/Shutterstock.com, pp. 8–9; Annette Shaff/Shutterstock.com, p. 10; Cheryl Thomas/Shutterstock.com, pp. 10–11; NadyZima_klgd/Shutterstock.com, pp. 12–13; DenisNata/Shutterstock.com, p. 13; tristan tan/Shutterstock.com, pp. 14–15; Daxiao Productions/Shutterstock.com, p. 16; kukuruxa/Shutterstock.com, pp. 16–17; PJ 5156/Shutterstock.com, pp. 18–19; Africa Studio/Shutterstock.com, p. 19; blewisphotography/Shutterstock.com, p. 20; Maria Dryfhout/Shutterstock.com, pp. 20–21; Monkey Business Images/Shutterstock.com, pp. 22–23; Suti Stock Photo/Shutterstock.com, p. 24; michaeljung/Shutterstock.com, pp. 24–25; defotoberg/Shutterstock.com, pp. 26–27; Michael Shake/Shutterstock.com, p. 27; Esin Deniz/Shutterstock.com, p. 28 (fish); Antanina/Shutterstock.com, p. 28 (cat); zorina_larisa/Shutterstock.com (design elements throughout).

Cover: Mariusz S. Jurgielewicz/Shutterstock.com (flowers); Menna/Shutterstock.com (oranges); Voyagerix/Shutterstock.com (cat); Maxim Tupikov/Shutterstock.com (leaves).